T002848Ξ

FREEDOM ON THE SEA

The True Story of the Civil War Hero Robert Smalls
and His Daring Escape to Freedom

WRITTEN BY
MICHAEL BOULWARE MOORE

ILLUSTRATED BY
BRYAN COLLIER

GODWINBOOKS

Henry Holt and Company • New York

Robert Smalls was twelve years old when he arrived in Charleston from his home in Beaufort, seventy miles away. For a Lowcountry boy raised on the water, it was quite the big city. Charleston had become the richest city in all of America from the skill and labor of enslaved people just like Robert.

Even as a boy, Robert was skilled in the ways of fishing and boats. When he first got to Charleston, he took odd jobs wherever he could. Eventually, he found work loading and unloading freight on an old 147-foot side-wheel steamer called the *Planter*. Over the years, he learned to sail the boat and advanced to the role of wheelman. Little did he know how critical that skill would be to his future and to history!

In April of 1861, when the Civil War broke out, Robert was in his early twenties. He was married and had two young children—Elizabeth and Robert Jr. His wife, Hannah, worked at a hotel called the Mills House. Robert and his family lived in an apartment above a barn on East Bay Street, not far from the docks. Although enslaved, they enjoyed some sense of independence living together.

To Robert, his family was the most important thing in his life. However, being enslaved meant that any one of them could be sold away at any time. Obviously, this troubled Robert greatly. He couldn't imagine living without them.

Robert was smart and full of ideas, so he began to think about how to keep his family together. He just *had* to figure something out!

Robert finally had an idea. He would persuade Samuel Kingman, the man who enslaved Hannah and their children, to allow him to buy their freedom. Already, Robert was allowed to save a dollar a week from his wages. With that money, he bought candy, fruit, and various things that he then sold on the docks. What if he could save every penny he made from this extra work? It was a long shot, but Robert thought this might be the way to buy his family's freedom!

Robert gathered his courage and approached Mr. Kingman with the proposal. And to his surprise and relief, Mr. Kingman agreed! Robert gave him a $100 down payment and promised to make regular payments until the total of $800 was paid. After that, his family would be free.

But Robert knew how hard it had been to earn the $100, and he couldn't be sure how long it would take to come up with the rest. So he kept thinking, trying to figure out an even better way to keep his family together. Finally, he had a new plan. It was extremely daring and extremely dangerous, and there was a real chance it might not work. But if he could pull it off, they would be forever free, and most importantly, they wouldn't have to wait for years.

Robert set about putting his plan into action. When the Civil War had begun, the *Planter* had been taken over by the Confederate military for its use. It mostly carried troops, cannons, and ammunition around the South Carolina waterways.

Robert noticed that sometimes at the end of the day, even though it was against the rules, the Confederate crew would leave the boat and often wouldn't return until the next day. That left Robert and the other enslaved crew there by themselves.

Robert knew that there was a Union blockade of warships in the waters just beyond Charleston Harbor. He also knew that if he could get there, he would be free. And if his family came with him, they would all be free.

Robert carefully watched the comings and goings of the *Planter*'s Confederate crew, and on May 12, 1862, when the crew left the ship, it was time to act! It was a cloudy, dark night when he backed the *Planter* off the dock and sailed away with sixteen enslaved people on board.

Robert's family and the other crew members and their families had all agreed to Robert's plan. They knew there was so much that could go wrong, but they were all determined to be free.

In Charleston Harbor, five forts stood between Robert and freedom. If the guards at any fort became suspicious about the *Planter* sailing so late at night, if Robert got one of the pass codes wrong, or if one of the guards noticed that the Confederate captain wasn't in charge, their dream of freedom would be lost.

Robert put on the long overcoat and straw top hat of the Confederate captain. He planned to mimic the captain's mannerisms so that in the dark and at a distance, he would look just like him.

For everyone on board, it was a life-or-death voyage. They would either free themselves or die trying. Before they left, they put dynamite in the bottom of the boat. If something went wrong, they would blow up the boat. One way or the other, slavery would be behind them.

Slowly, carefully, the *Planter* sailed to the first fort, then the second, third, and fourth. After each fort, there was a rise and fall of emotions. Fear and anxiety as they approached, and then relief and happiness as the guards allowed them to pass. And when they sailed toward the next fort, the cycle began again.

After passing all but one, the biggest and most dangerous fort was ahead. But just past that was . . . freedom.

Fort Sumter was the place where the Civil War began. It was the biggest fort in Charleston Harbor. It had the largest cannons, and its walls stood fifty feet high. As they approached Fort Sumter, Robert felt the sweat beading on his forehead, trickling down the back of his neck, stinging his eyes . . .

Just as the first rays of the new sun were coming up over the horizon, Robert blew the pass code on the ship's whistle. And then he mopped his brow and waited. Why didn't they respond? Was something wrong? Maybe the guards could now see Robert clearly. Maybe they could tell he wasn't the captain.

Finally, Robert heard it. The guard shouted, "Pass the *Planter*!" They still had to sail past the reach of Fort Sumter's cannons, but they were relieved to be on the way with clear water ahead! At that moment, Robert allowed himself to feel a bubble of joy. They might make it! They might all be free!

Little did he know that the most dangerous threat was just ahead.

After the *Planter* was beyond the reach of Fort Sumter's cannons, Robert quickly steered the ship south toward the Union blockade. The sun was almost up now. The sky was red and orange with hope and freedom. Robert had thought about every detail, and so far, things had worked.

As the *Planter* sailed full steam ahead toward the Union ships, Robert realized something that made his heart sink. He had forgotten one crucial detail, one that could spoil their dreams and even cost them their lives.

Because here was the *Planter*, one of the largest Confederate ships, steaming briskly—and unannounced—toward the Union blockade with an enormous enemy flag flying high above it. Robert imagined the looks on the faces of the Union sailors as this menacing Confederate ship sailed straight for them. No doubt they were readying for a confrontation that could be deadly for all. Robert realized that their survival was now in greater jeopardy than it had been at any other time on this tension-filled journey.

Unbeknownst to Robert, Hannah had anticipated just such a threat and had sewn together a few white bedsheets and brought them on board. Quickly, they lowered the Confederate flag and raised the white sheets of surrender.

The Union sailors held their fire and allowed the *Planter* to approach. As Robert and the rest of the group stepped onto the USS *Onward*, everyone was overcome with emotion. They had dreamed about winning their freedom, but were some of the very, very few enslaved people who had actually achieved it.

The commander of the blockade, Admiral S. F. Du Pont, greeted Robert. Smiling broadly and pointing to the *Planter*, Robert said, "We thought old Uncle Abe could have some use for this!"

And as of that moment on May 13, 1862, Robert, Hannah, Elizabeth, and Robert Jr. were free!

Dear Readers,

In my heart and soul, I carry the profound connection I have with my great-great-grandfather Robert Smalls. From the moment I unveiled his bust at Tabernacle Baptist Church in 1976, his story became an inseparable part of my life. I have been lifting his name ever since, driven by a deep desire to share his inspiring journey with the world.

Robert Smalls's legacy is a testament to triumph over adversity, a story that resonates with people from all walks of life. From slavery to freedom, from daring escape to respected statesmanship, his life embodies the indomitable human spirit. I believe his story holds valuable lessons that can bridge divides and unite us in hope and determination.

Immersed in his life's tale, I found myself profoundly inspired. It has led me to run for the very same seat in Congress that he once served, living out my inspiration from this remarkable man.

This book is a celebration of resilience, hope, and boundless potential. Through its pages, I aim to ignite a flame of hope and progress, fostering unity and inspiring future generations to lead with compassion, courage, and conviction.

I am deeply grateful to those who have supported me on this journey and to my family, whose connection to Robert Smalls fuels my dedication.

Let us join hands in celebration of Robert Smalls's extraordinary life and embrace the power of storytelling to bridge the gaps between us. May his story continue to shine brightly, igniting the spark of inspiration in every heart it touches.

With sincerest regards,
Michael Boulware Moore

To my cherished first grandchild, Sasha, the great-great-great-great-
granddaughter of Robert Smalls, and to all of your future siblings and cousins.
May his remarkable story inspire and uplift you, guiding you to even greater
heights than it has guided me. With all my love and pride.
—M. B. M.

I dedicate this book to Chandler and Christian Scott for
participating as main character models in this book project.
Thank you for helping me honor the legacy of Robert Smalls.
—B. C.

Henry Holt and Company, *Publishers since 1866*
Henry Holt® is a registered trademark of Macmillan Publishing Group, LLC
120 Broadway, New York, NY 10271 • mackids.com

Text copyright © 2024 by Michael Boulware Moore. Art copyright © 2024 by Bryan Collier.
All rights reserved.

Our books may be purchased in bulk for promotional, educational, or business use. Please contact your local
bookseller or the Macmillan Corporate and Premium Sales Department at (800) 221-7945 ext. 5442 or by
email at MacmillanSpecialMarkets@macmillan.com.

Library of Congress Cataloging-in-Publication Data is available.

First edition, 2024
Book design by Mina Chung
The art for this book was created with watercolor and collage on cold-press 300 lb Arches watercolor paper.
Printed in China by 1010 Printing International Limited, Kwun Tong, Hong Kong

ISBN 978-1-250-81835-5
1 3 5 7 9 10 8 6 4 2